Clip-Art
Sentence
Sermons

Clip-Art Sentence Sermons
for Church Publications

George W. Knight, Compiler
Howard Paris, Illustrator

BAKER BOOK HOUSE
Grand Rapids, Michigan 49506

Copyright 1986 by
Baker Book House Company

ISBN: 0-8010-5475-3

Sixth printing, March 1992

Printed in the United States of America

Contents

Thought-provoking Messages for Readers on the Run   7

Subject, **number**, page

Action, **1-5**, 11
Adversity, **6**, 13
Advice, **7-9**, 13
Character, **10**, 15
Church, **11**, 15
Excuses, **12**, 15
Experience, **13, 14**, 17
Failure, **15-17**, 17
Faith, **18**, 19
Flexibility, **19**, 19
Friendship, **20-25**, 19
Goals, **26**, 23
Gossip, **27, 28**, 23
Grace, **29**, 25
Habits, **30, 31**, 25
Humor, **23-40**, 25
Interpersonal
    Relationships, **41-45**, 31

Leisure, **46, 47**, 33
Marriage, **48, 49**, 33
Money, **50-55**, 35
Opportunity, **56, 57**, 37
Parenthood, **58-60**, 39
Prayer, **61, 62**, 41
Progress, **63**, 41
Responsibility, **64**, 41
Self-improvement, **65**, 43
Sermons, **66-68**, 43
Service, **69**, 45
Success, **70-74**, 45
Talk, **75-77**, 47
Television, **78**, 49
Tomorrow, **79**, 49
Witnessing, **80**, 49
Work, **81-92**, 51
Worry, **93-96**, 57

Thought-provoking Messages for Readers on the Run

More and more churches are waking up to the great potential of the church newsletter. Mailed regularly into the homes of *all* members, it can serve as a silent spokesman for the values which the church proclaims. Prospects, interested visitors, even church members who attend irregularly or not at all—all these target groups can be reached effectively week after week through this publication.

As they become aware of the newsletter's potential, churches are searching for suitable materials to make these publications more appealing to a broader range of readers. The sentence sermons in this book are designed first to attract attention and then to deliver an enriching message very quickly. Even the person who scans the newsletter can take these messages in. Each sentence sermon is crisp, light, and eye-catching—specifically designed to catch the attention of the reader on the run.

All these sentence sermons are copyright-free to local churches. Just clip them out of the book and paste them down on your newsletter layout sheet for quick-and-easy reproduction by copying machine, electronic stencil, or offset press.

My thanks to Howard Paris of Mableton, Georgia, for creating the cartoon-style illustrations used throughout the book. A professional cartoonist for more than thirty-five years, Howard has captured just the effect we were looking for with these sentence sermons— serious messages with a light-hearted approach.

George W. Knight

Clip-Art Sentence Sermons

Do It Now!

Today is seldom too early; tomorrow is usually too late.

The Future: A Definition

The future is that time when you'll wish you had done what you aren't doing now.

How to Help Out

The best kind of helping hand is the one at the end of your arm.

Keep It Burning

It is much easier to keep the fire burning than to rekindle it after it has gone out.

Great Expectations

It's futile to look for your ship to come in unless you have sent one out.

Unseen Obstacles

The ladder of life is full of splinters—most of which you don't see until you start sliding down.

Absolutely Free

If at first you don't succeed— you'll get plenty of advice.

Good Advice

Ask enough people and you'll always find someone who advises you to do exactly what you planned to do in the first place.

Pleasurable Giving

Medicine and advice are two things more pleasant to give than to receive.

Holding Power

Ability may get you to the top, but only character will keep you there.

A Busy Hive

The church is a hive for workers, not a nest for drones.

How to Test an Excuse

Never give an excuse for yourself that you wouldn't accept from another person.

The All-knowing Age

It's too bad all of life's problems can't hit us when we're 18—the stage of life when we know everything.

The Value of Experience

There's nothing like experience; it helps you recognize a mistake the second time you make it.

Accumulated Wisdom

Think of failure as an opportuni-ly to try again, wiser than before.

Learning in Life

Learn from the mistakes of others. You won't live long enough to make them all yourself.

Imperfection's By-product

One nice thing about being imperfect is the joy it brings to other people.

Faith and the Rain

Prayer is asking for rain, and faith is taking an umbrella.

Hardened Minds

Some minds are like concrete—all mixed up and permanently set.

How to Lose Friends

The problem with being a grouch is that you have to make a new set of friends every few weeks.

Nice Guy

A really nice guy is a person who has never heard the story before.

Happy Saver

The happiest person on earth is the one who saves friends.

A True Friend

A true friend is a person who remembers your birthday but forgets how many you've had.

How to Lose Friends

One sure way to lose friends is to win all the arguments.

Remember Your Friends

Be nice to your friends. If it weren't for them, you would be a total stranger.

Destination: Anywhere

The person who doesn't know where he's going usually gets there in record time.

Did You Hear . . . ?

The best way to get people to believe anything is to *whisper* it.

The Spread Thickens

Rumor is one thing that gets thicker as you spread it.

Saved by Grace

God loves us the way we are—but he cares too much to leave us that way.

Both Easy and Hard

Bad habits are like a comfortable bed—easy to get into and hard to get out of.

Temper and Pride

Temper gets most of us in trouble, and pride keeps us there.

Happiness Galore

If we learn to laugh at ourselves, we will always have something to make us happy.

Definition of an Expert

An expert is an ordinary person a hundred miles from home.

Life from the Sidelines

It's always easy to see both sides of an issue you're not particularly concerned about.

Grand Central Station

A hospital room is a place where friends of the patient go to talk to other friends of the patient.

Inexpensive Item

About the only thing free of charge these days is a run-down battery.

Fertile Field

All it takes to grow healthy grass is a crack in the driveway.

Definition of a Foot

A foot is a device for finding furniture in the dark.

The Ideal Guest

A perfect guest always makes his host feel right at home.

Frustration with a Capital F

Frustration is not having anyone to blame but yourself.

An Impossible Act

People with clenched fists can't shake hands.

Closing the Distance

Laughter is the shortest distance between two people.

Artful Conversation

Diplomacy is the art of telling others they have open minds instead of holes in their heads.

Exit for Happiness

Some people bring happiness wherever they go . . . some others *when* they go.

A Useless Activity

No matter how long you nurse a grudge, it won't get better.

Respectable Inactivity

The nice thing about quiet meditation is that it makes doing nothing look very respectable.

Too Much Work

Work is a fine thing if it doesn't take too much of your leisure time.

A Good Marriage

A happy marriage exists when the couple is as deeply in love as it is in debt.

Strange Transformation

The problem with marriage is that we fall in love with a *personality* but we end up living with a *character*.

No Compliment

Remember the time when "sound as a dollar" was a real compliment?

Good Timing

Statistics prove that the best time to buy anything is a year ago.

Short Season

The best way to shorten the winter is to borrow some money that you have to pay back in the spring.

No Free Ride

If you get something for a song, watch out for the accompaniment.

Inflationary Lesson

Every time history repeats itself, the price of the lesson goes up.

Fundamental Economics

Money certainly is a medium of exchange. A medium amount of it won't exchange for very much these days.

Tough Grass

The greener grass next door is probably just as hard to cut.

Making Opportunities

A wise person always makes more opportunities than he finds.

Hereditary Wrinkles

Wrinkles are hereditary; parents get them from their children.

A Pedestrian Defined

A pedestrian is a person who has two cars, a spouse, and one or more teenage children.

They Do as Parents Do

Parents should remember that children will probably follow their example rather than their advice.

Watch Your Prayers

Don't pray for rain if you intend to complain about the mud.

Great Expectations

Too many Christians expect a million-dollar answer to a ten-cent prayer.

Progress Without Change

Most people are in favor of progress; it's change they can't stand.

The Flip Side of Grace

Count your obligations—
Name them one by one—
And it will surprise you
What the Lord wants done.

No Time Left

Give your efforts to improving yourself, and you'll have little time left for criticizing others.

Too Much In-between

The ends of some sermons, like the covers on some books, are too far apart.

After the Sermon

A "religious awakening" is what takes place after the preacher ends the sermon.

The Speaker's Prayer

Lord, fill my mouth with
worthwhile stuff,
And stop me when
I've said enough.

The Power of Service

Life is like tennis; the player who serves well has a good chance of winning.

Tempting Rest

The road to success is lined with many tempting parking spaces.

The Ladder Barrier

All that stands between some people and the top of the ladder is the ladder.

Sweat Success

Success is sweet, but it requires a lot of sweat.

The Route to Success

One thing common to most success stories is the alarm clock.

Lined Up on the Dock

The problem with success is that when your ship comes in, most of your friends and relatives are standing on the dock.

A Sensible Rule

Always try to stop talking before people stop listening.

Dropping a Conversation

It's all right to hold a conversation—but you should let go of it now and then.

Sound Economics

The reason why talk is cheap is that the supply exceeds the demand.

Yesterday's Annoyances

Do you remember when the only thing that annoyed you about television was poor reception?

A Hectic Day

If tomorrow should ever arrive, it would be the busiest day of the year.

Barren Witness

Some Christians are like the Arctic rivers—frozen at the mouth.

Those Mondays!

Monday certainly is a tough way to spend one-seventh of your life.

Fruitful Waiting

It's good to wait on the Lord—as long as you're busy while you wait.

How to Kill Time

The best way to kill time is to work it to death.

Thinking of Plowing

Every farmer knows he can't plow a field by turning it over in his mind.

Success Before Work?

The only place where success comes before work is in the dictionary.

Energetic Work

God put work into our lives; He expects us to put life into our work.

Overworked?

Most people are never too busy to stop and tell you how busy they are.

No Competition

Making an honest living should be easy; there's so little competition these days.

Stages of Accomplishment

Every great accomplishment has three distinct stages: (1) It's impossible, (2) it's difficult, and (3) it's done.

Don't Interrupt!

People who say that something is impossible should not interrupt those who are managing to get it done.

Stretching a Job

It takes some people a long time to get nothing done.

Don't Stop Plowing

Pray for a good harvest, but keep on plowing.

The Shadow

Worry always gives a little thing a big shadow.

How to Sleep Well

How you handle your problems by day has a lot to do with how you sleep at night.

Energy-consuming Worry

A day of worry burns more energy than a week of work.

Prescription for Worry

Blessed is the person who is too busy to worry during the day and too sleepy to worry at night.